HENRY'S FATE

& Other Poems

HENRY'S FATE

& Other Poems, 1967–1972

JOHN BERRYMAN — 1914–1972

NEW YORK

FARRAR, STRAUS AND GIROUX

1977

FIRST PRINTING, 1977

Printed in the United States of America
Published simultaneously in Canada
by McGraw-Hill Ryerson Ltd., Toronto
DESIGNED BY HERB JOHNSON

Library of Congress Cataloging in Publication Data

Berryman, John, 1914–1972.
Henry's fate & other poems, 1967–1972.

I. Title.
PS3503.E744H4   1977   811'.5'4   76-52950

Acknowledgment is made to *The New Yorker*,
in which six of the uncollected Dream Songs originally appeared;
to *The* (London) *Times Literary Supplement*, in which six poems
appeared; to *The Atlantic,* in which two poems appeared; to *Arion, The
Harvard Advocate,* and *The Virginia Quarterly Review,* in each of
which one poem appeared; and to *The American Poetry Review,*
in which thirteen poems appeared

CONTENTS

II

III FRAGMENTS AND UNFINISHED POEMS

IV

Introduction by John Haffenden

This volume of poems, written between 1967 and 1972 (the last poem but one having been written within forty-eight hours of his death), represents only a fraction of Berryman's unpublished and uncollected work. There are several hundred unpublished Dream Songs, and as many more miscellaneous poems. There is a harvest of essays and papers on Shakespeare, including a critical edition of *King Lear* virtually completed many years ago. In his last year of life, Berryman received an award from the National Endowment for the Humanities to proceed with and coordinate his biographical study of Shakespeare. He died before he could complete the project, but enough manuscript survives to substantiate his claims to consideration in that area. There is also a volume of dream analysis, worked on (but unfinished) in 1954–55. There are several plays, and one or two stories and essays not included in *The Freedom of the Poet* (1976). There are numerous letters, and diaries which in many places are of a kind that may preclude publication for some years. Berryman once remarked that he hoped to be remembered as a man who worked hard. The evidence for that wish is assured survival.

The time is not yet ripe for a complete edition of his works. For this volume it has been thought wisest to select poems from Berryman's later years which are worthy of publication in a volume of their own. Many poems in this selection were written at the time Berryman was working on the volumes that emerged as *Love & Fame* and *Delusions, Etc*. Let us suppose that each poem was at some point considered for those volumes and put aside. We may still not presume reasons for their omission, which might have been those of length, subject, or even incongruence to the basic themes and structure of those volumes. In the light of Berryman's recognized standards and procedures, we judge that many poems which Berryman refused or forgot to publish are of a quality high enough to stand with his published work.

Part I of this volume, which consists entirely of uncollected Dream Songs, gives occasion for special pleasure. The most outstanding achievement of Berryman's published career was that of 77 *Dream Songs* (1964) and *His Toy, His Dream, His Rest* (1968), which together earned him several awards, including the Pulitzer Prize and the National Book Award for poetry. As early as 1964, Berryman was already projecting that, if a further volume of Dream Songs were to be published after *His Toy, His Dream, His Rest*, it might be called *Addenda* or *Parerga*. In May 1968 an interview with Berryman in the Minneapolis *Tribune* revealed that the "two volumes of Dream Songs have taken Berryman's main character, Henry, as far as he will go, the poet said. Not all the songs about Henry are in the books, Berryman said, but if there is a third volume, it will be up to the reader to fit those poems in among the published ones." Lastly, in a letter of June 1970 to J. M. Linebarger, Berryman seemed to exclude uncollected Dream Songs from the work known as *The Dream Songs:* "None of them . . . will ever be attached to the poem by me, and in fact I may just leave them to be published after my death." What in these statements was concessive may now be seen as permissive. But why draw a line at 1967 and exclude from the present volume all unpublished or uncollected Dream Songs written before then? The answer is that Berryman had nearly completed *His Toy, His Dream, His Rest* in the late summer of 1967. He was working then from a bulk of poems which were written up to and including the period of his Guggenheim residence in Dublin, which ended that summer. The Songs now printed take off from that point. The first group, written in Europe, Berryman never had occasion to put into typed form. And so too with the others, printed here in chronological order so far as it can be determined, and written mostly in 1968 and some in the two following years. As far as Berryman himself was concerned, *The Dream Songs* was a completed venture, and it is true that, as he told Linebarger, most of these Songs were written "just out of habit." They were penned as chance seemed to dictate. As to Dream Songs written perhaps earlier in 1967, and in all previous years, it is not possible to say, with the same kind of assurance as of this group, that Berryman did not choose to omit them as inferior or redundant.

The decision to include the unfinished poem "Proemio" and the draft fragments of "Washington in Love" has been made for the following reasons. The version of "Washington in Love" that Berryman published in *Delusions, Etc.* (1972) consisted of 7 discrete lines of poetry, an elliptical sketch of George Washington's life. The discovery of the draft version of this poem, dating from early January 1970, has disclosed interesting features of its original scope and intentions. Rummaging through the attic of Berryman's house in another bitterly cold Minnesota January—1975—I came across this Ur-*Washington in Love* in the form of sixteen note pages clipped together. They are reproduced here just as Berryman wrote them, complete with disjunctions and occasional lack of punctuation. I feel that they merit attention as throwing light on Berryman's methods of working, insights and style, as parts of an ambitious, if unfinished, poem.

"Proemio," which dates from 10–22 June 1971, was, strictly speaking, to have been the proem to a much longer work, what Berryman himself referred to as "my third epic"—after, that is to say, *Homage to Mistress Bradstreet* and *The Dream Songs*. The subject of this new major poem was to be itself the poet's quest for "a subject," resolving itself—at once fulfilled and abandoned—as a concentration on the poet's three children and their futures. *Homage to Mistress Bradstreet* had been written, as he himself described it (in 1971), "for a distant future"; *The Dream Songs*, "for the present & some future"; and this latest poem—presumably to have been called *The Children*—"for the present merely," the next ten years at most. Another note indicates something more of the poet's plans for this projected work: "It will include instructions to them [the children] on every subject I feel sufficiently strongly about and either know inside-out or am wholly perplext by." The "Proemio" printed here would seem to have been substantially completed as a prologue to the body of the poem, and is especially interesting as a new departure for Berryman toward mock-heroic blank verse. At a time when Berryman was working on the novel *Recovery*, on a life of Shakespeare, and a life of Christ, as well as continuing with other poems, it is not surprising that this new venture made no further progress. In 1971, Berryman was a sick man: the years of alcohol and unrelenting study and creativity had taken their toll.

Poems printed here have been collated, wherever possible, with holograph versions. Occasionally Berryman indicated, by his usual practice of a wavy underline, that a word or phrase was to be changed in future drafts: in the few instances where no alternatives were provided, first thoughts must inevitably be the last.

These are probably not the last of the later Berryman poems. Judging from the author's sometimes fine carelessness ("Old Codger Henry" was found, for example, on a scrap of envelope tucked away in an edition of Coleridge), other poems will come to light, from behind bookcases, dust jackets, and other spots of abandonment, hiding, or repose.

"Why write?" John Berryman asked himself once. His list of reasons was extensive: sublimation, habit, boredom, rage, self-reform, *need;* to entertain, to *praise,* to get X into bed, to "justify," express self-pity, gain prestige, get promotion, *not* to disappoint friends; money, fame, posterity. All these reasons applied at one time or another to Berryman's own career. One notable omission from the list (perhaps because he took it wholly for granted) was inspiration, which he rarely lacked.

He was a man who lived, for many years, a life absolute for poetry. He spent literally years on end worrying form and style toward that point where thought and feeling accord. He was a man who honored his literary debts—to Yeats, Pound, Auden, Stevens, Rilke—for perhaps too long. It took nearly twenty years of apprenticeship before he could write a major poem, *Homage to Mistress Bradstreet*, his first outstanding critical success.

For the years of his youth and into early manhood, he was nervous, intense, wildly excitable, a snob in poetry, but always alive with what Delmore Schwartz called his "mad charm." For perhaps most of the years of his mature achievement (dating from the early 1950s), he suffered and caused others to suffer from his alcoholism. He lusted in many ways, for sexual dominion, which was often achieved, and for fame, which came late. Possessed of the relentless conviction—nurtured first by his mother, later by his mentors and fellows—that he could eventually accomplish wonderful work, he came in the end to make purchase of a mirage.

> *Henry was programmed for happiness.*
> *What happened O, O bloody friends?*
> *Hoho, heehee.*

He was always fired with knowledge of poetry and with ideas about poetry, but his ambivalence and nervous apprehension could be extreme. Although he could put his feet up among any number of poets, he himself held back from committing his own work to print. When he did so, it was with a combination of arrogance and terror. While the day-to-day affairs of his life foundered around him, he invariably managed to summon from somewhere enough energy for his writing tasks. Even when admitted to the hospital in a state of acute exhaustion or alcoholism, he would soon be sitting up in bed at work on poems or notes. He always retained an energetic, in some ways overweening, will-to-fame. His high valuation of his own gifts, given an access of indignation at real or imagined slights, made success itself suspect. His emergence to fame exposed him to himself even more nakedly. Drinking and the inability to rest from his labors broke down his body again and again.

> *Sober Henry hid his glass,*
> *Henry would have to be sober from here out.*

> *His voluntary drug makes his brain swim,*
> *he holds things that aren't here,*
> *sees what never was. It's clear*
> *Henry can't make it.*

It was not uncommon to find him slumped asleep in a chair as the small hours gained shadows, a student or a fan in attendance. By 1971, when he was a recovering alcoholic, he gained a measure of wry self-awareness in his dealings with flatterers and hangers-on. A diary entry from this period reads: "(Am I master of my emotions?) *To some extent*—witness my bearing with the young writer yesterday for 1 ½ hours and ushering him politely out *alive*."

He was in fact a kind of Philoctetes. Periodically, his own form of abscess—the grievous knowledge of his father's suicide, and his own alcoholism and insomnia—would burst from him in pain. When acclaim, success, and authority were at last assured him, when large sums of money could be his for the effort of hoofing the lecture platforms of America, his mental and physical deterioration was such that he could not go on.

> *But on the whole, no, he would not live on:*
> *the possibilities of the punishment is such:*
> *OW.*
> *Yes, he's up against it for* him. *Let Henry begone,*
> *yet let the loves & good guys live, from now*
> *till they get tired of it, man.*

He wrote, toward the end of his life, "You've got to exaggerate / even grief to reach the ear in-turned of man." Yet, we must know, he had a notion of what Edward Young meant when he spoke of grief as grandeur in disguise.

> An alcoholic [he wrote in 1971] is not more responsible for his vices than the gangrene victim for his stench. Both offend, innocent, feeling ineradicable guilt, with shame and rage.

He never subscribed to the facile idea that the vices of the man might be virtues to the poet. Suffering might help the poetry, but sin would not. One of his worst burdens was the feeling that being a poet could not excuse his transgressions as a man.

In June 1955, a low point in his career, he wrote an epitaph for himself:

> He was a poet. To earn a living—instead of scrounging as he should have done—he lectured on subjects he knew nothing about to students incapable of learning anything. He was obliged to live in the capitals of the greatest empire the world has ever seen, at the supreme moment of its prosperity; could afford to write very little; and died.

The self-pity here was real, but the quantity of self-deprecation was absurd. At just this period in his life, he was about to embark on a work that has become a landmark in mid-century American literature, *The Dream Songs*. The notion that he lectured on subjects he knew nothing about was also ridiculous. He was a man of immense learning which, while it could lend itself to display, yet gave a tremendous depth and range of themes on solid showing, knots of knowledge to tie into his verse. It is important to recognize, for example, the urgent need for understanding that informed his biblical studies.

The style and matter of *The Dream Songs* has given rise to much dissent. Professors are set at odds and students sometimes stumped. Throughout the writing, Berryman regarded the Songs rather in the way Cardinal Newman felt about one of his works of interpretation, as tentative and empirical. Critics throw up guesses as to the real identities of Henry and of Henry's friend, the two chief characters of the Songs. Berryman himself joked that no one had yet identified Henry's friend correctly. It may be important to know, for example, that on 6 April 1960 Berryman noted that " 'Mr Bones' is *Death*, Henry's friend—who at the end takes him offstage." The syntax here suggests that Mr Bones, Death, and Henry's friend are all one and the same person, a tantalizing concept. It is also important to understand, however, that even this identification never solidified in the poet's mind, which did not take a schematic or categorical turn. Pondering the problem, Berryman himself subscribed to the view that people are whole, unique beings, not to be explained, for example, in terms only of id, ego, and superego. What was important to *The Dream Songs*, his major work, was to dramatize the vicissitudes of the sense of identity. Henry may well be called the mid-century man *en biscuit*, but Henry is not a type. Eileen Simpson, Berryman's first wife, presented her findings on this very question in a talk to the New Jersey Psychological Association on 17 February 1951. She gained her master's degree at New York University with a dissertation, "Poets' Responses to the Rorschach Test," and was careful to maintain that her findings "did not uncover a universal poet type."

F. Scott Fitzgerald claimed that all his characters, filtered through his own mind and personality, belonged to the consciousness of the race, and that he could not keep the truth out of his work. The same might be said of Berryman vis-à-vis Henry's role in the Dream Songs, pausing only to exclude the conceit of Fitzgerald's remark.

The Dream Songs have been criticized for their abstruseness, their allusiveness, and their general incomprehensibility. Louise Bogan called Berryman the enemy of the English language for 77 *Dream Songs*. One conceives of an accumulation of, to borrow a phrase from St.-John Perse, "la literie du songe et la litière du savoir." It is true that the Songs are dense with learning, with private references, with dream associations, with idioms and syntax that some may feel barbaric. It is also true that the Songs *work—*cry, laugh, exalt, and exert themselves to animate all aspects of being and feeling, from the doting delight of "Twissy went poo on the potty. We all have our achievements" to the savage imponderables of despair and death.

> *Often I desired to die. I did not love death.*
> *I hated happenings, and was afraid.*
> *Take off events & fear . . .*
>
> *The fury of the body growing old,*
> *hurting, humiliated. Without thought*
> *of anything new to come*
> *magnificent, or even desired*
> *Ha! hell.*

W. H. Auden suggested, about ten years ago, that Hölderlin and Smart expressed themselves crazily because they themselves were dotty, not from any deliberate, if bizarre, use of language. This argument implies a discretion between language and thought, and has to be contested. An arrangement of words—a sentence or a line of verse—is an applied structure of knowledge and personality. The "real thing" may be difficult to define, but can always be perceived. The truth of poetry is as susceptible of positive identification by qualities of "voice" as a man by his fingerprints or a horse by its chestnuts. Imitation provides perhaps a secondary index of success. When Philip Toynbee reviewed 77 *Dream Songs*, he incorporated his own parodies of the Songs alongside the real thing. Berryman stared at the article in disbelief, puzzled as to the provenance of the unfamiliar stanzas and then angered at such treatment. But the false owes everything to the real and, in its turn, gives the real new stature. A borrowing is a bouquet. The shadow admits to the sun.

What, in the final analysis, must be stressed among the positive aspects of Berryman's life and work is the capacity for friendship, love, and fun. When in 1970, for example, he wrote an angry letter to *The Nation* complaining of misrepresentation and obtuseness in a review of *Love & Fame*, he expressed delight at a comparison of his work with that of Lowell, Roethke, Schwartz, Jarrell, Elizabeth Bishop, and Wilbur: "The company is positively bracing! My pals!" His capacity for love and friendship, as Lowell, Meredith, and Bellow have witnessed, was total. To a lady who dared suggest jealousy between poets he replied with two lines of verse:

> *Lady, all poets, all few, love each other up.*
> *This profession is scary. We are friends.*

Similarly, in September 1963, he declared:

> *Some of my best friends drink . . . ,*
> *screw men, have lovely bastards, on the whole*
> *(except long since) are unacceptable.*
>   *And I love them.*

It is difficult to speak to the subject of anyone's sense of humor, but Berryman's spanned a wild range, from subtle irony and wit through to burlesque. Take a xenophobic extravagance:

> *. . . all foreigners*
> *Except at home the Japanese*
> *are strictly for the turds and wessels. Why*
> *pretend? They are & are as I have said.*

Often, as William Meredith has suggested, *The Dream Songs* give the impression of laughter in the face of humiliation, despair, and death. Once, on a "recreational-therapy" outing from the hospital, Berryman was among a group of patients watching the movie *Camelot*. Berryman was bored to death and wanted a cigarette. Terence Collins describes what happened: "During the song 'What Do the Simple Folk Do' Berryman supplied, in his overly loud voice

and from the balcony, a new line in perfect time with the song—
'They screw, they screw.' The result was some laughter throughout
the theatre and a great deal of embarrassment to the depressed
menopausal ladies who were along on the outing."

Berryman embodied in his life the truth of his own phrase, "The
happier you get the worse you feel." It is this sort of ambivalence
that Berryman's work portrays, as he himself recognized when
introducing *The Dream Songs* at Harvard University in 1966:
"Prepare to weep, ladies and gentlemen. Saul Bellow and I almost
kill ourselves laughing about the Dream Songs and various chapters
in his novels, but other people feel bad. Are you all ready to feel
bad?"

His life and work also incorporated a theodicy, as Christopher
Ricks has indicated. Berryman's theodicy is based, I believe, on a
text from St. Paul (Rom. 5:20) referred to in Dream Song 20,
"The Secret of the Wisdom":

> *. . . We hear the more*
> *sin has increast, the more*
> *grace has been caused to abound.*

He was a man who participated readily in *eros*, but who had to
progress toward the recognition and expression of *agape*. One of
the simplest and most moving of his documents was written toward
the end of his life, and is worth quotation in full:

A Morning Prayer

According to Thy Will. Thank you for everything that was good
in me yesterday, and forgive everything that was not. Thank you
for the great rescues of my life & for the marvellous good luck that
has mostly attended me. Enlighten me as to the nature of Christ.
Strengthen my gratitude & awe into confident reliance & love of
Thee. Increase my humility & patience. Reconcile me to my
sufferings. Make tranquil my nerves. Bring Kate & me to a fuller
understanding & a deeper love. Keep me active today, & grant me
accuracy & insight in my work. Preserve me today from the desire
for a drink & if it comes enable me to lay it aside unsatisfied.
Enlighten me on the problem of personal immortality. Bless
everybody in the world, especially some of them, Thou knowest
whom. Amen.

I Uncollected Dream Songs

CANAL smell. City that lies on the sea like a cork
of stone & gold, manifold throng your ghosts
of murdered & distraught.
St Mark's remains came here covered with pork,
stolen from Islam. Freedom   & power, the Venetian hosts
cluttered blue seas where they sought

the wingèd lion on the conquered gates.
Doge followed Doge down down, the city floated.
Vassals drencht maps.
Fat popes & emperors to the high altar, hates
soothed into peace here. Nothing went unnoted
by the Patriarch perhaps

for a thousand years, when Henry struck his forehead
over his strange eyes & his monstrous beard
ah-ing 'This is too much.'
Canal smell, the Byzantine beauty of the dead,
with lovers arm in arm by the basin, weird
to Henry as such.

Many bore uncomplaining their lives pained
so long and in such weather. Henry complained.
All a Venetian June
the sun raged down on stone & water. Gondoliers slept
thro' midday on to four. Man was inept
against the sun, and soon

humid Henry took boat up the Grand Canal
where the breeze & the palaces refreshed him, pal,
palaces bold & demure.
Churches in dozens chose his attention; closed
like Rome's some fourteen years ago. He dozed,
dreaming of the stupendous & impure

success of men on these islands, hard on men
but easy now the fabulous city again
with Stellio in command
& vino & Scellio at the bar is being good
to almost prostrate foreigners full of gratitude
for the power here, brain & hand.

LEGMAN assman bustman, abominable Henry
wandered thro' France & Italy agog:
my God what visible places.
Everywhere he studied with both his eyes the faces
of those whose fates were his, like a Sligo bog
to be cut & burnt, or be

flourisht amongst great clouds for a long time
ah next San Marco choiring, who was cut off
just ere he finisht his work,
Henry's destiny? He fought it tooth & rime
country to country, hanging on. When he's had enough
he'll mount into the dark

but not (praise Serenissimo) until
tranquil in Athens to the final touch
he takes his restless labour.
O he is not working as at the mill
nor is he working yet for any neighbour
save two, whom with the future he counts on much.

OUT of this city musical where Henry is obscure
in a grand hotel upon a casual canal,
near Ponte Goldoni,
he'll stream by train to an international festival
to perform his tricks, which he can hardly endure
but then he did agree.

Then on to London, to perform more tricks.
Photographers, reporters once again.
Then the Aegean.
A busy summer for a solitudinem of men,
who wisheth pax. The fellow's in a fix
and he did it all himself.

O long ago he stretched forth a palm
open to the world; he's turned it upside down,
who wisheth pax.
Tired, a little, Henry opted for Athenian calm
but he will be sorry to leave this town,
cat, criminal, fox.

Henry, staggering, elderly, black, nearly fell off the Acropolis,
it is so damned old high.
Visions of the feet of Pericles
retrieved him, though the Parthenon is empty.
The statues are all in the National Museum
and London, etc, & melted down.

Athene, grace my age with wisdom, please you.
Let not my cluttered & tragic youth dispel
my radiant babyhood
which I may now resume, like peek-a-boo,
I admit the islands now, like Lesbos, spell
me silence like food,

like the strange fish we lately ate, my dear.
Flesh strong & good, also with mayonnaise
in Greek.
Your worship's interrupted, Henry's a mere
admirer, who do not kneel down & prays
& who is far to seek.

His inspiration lost, o'ercast, his Grecian café
shut for a holiday, he strove to say
'Hurrah' to his lady cat
upon her all-returning good birthday
when she'll be twenty-eight.
And there is no substitute for that.

27's too soon, too immature,
29 verges horribly on 30:
OW!
Two lengthy years—will still they see her pure?
as such things go, in the world, which is so dirty?
which she will not allow

but holds her standard to the mountain-top
which Henry once deserted but no more
O ho ho ho
we parleyed in a foul-mouth'd dialogue
last night: thunders over the high theatre applaud:
let's knock it off & go back home to the dog.

GULLS chains voices bells: honey we're home.
I don't care whether they cremate Henry or not.
His labour of travel is done
He came upon some shore one time like foam
but had to set out again or rot
with his life on him like a ton.

Unlike this feverish voyaging where new facts turned up
hourly, monthly, among stale voyagers
mostly American
loud rich & rude & petty, whom God also will call to a stop
without the languages, bitches without their curs.
Rats across the Quai Voltaire run, can

frighten you honey at dusk or an Arab Street:
we knew that: Henry had the wit to be afraid
and so my dear love were you.
The ship bangs in. We relax in defeat,
stiffen to the new acquaintances to be made
& the sky over our graves is blue.

Henry under construction was Henry indeed:
gigantic cranes faltered under the load,
spark-showers from the welding played
with daylight, crew after crew
replaced each other like Kings, all done anew
Daily, to the horror of the gathering crowd
which gazed in a silence of awe or sobbed aloud.

The structure huge mounted apace. Some sang,
others in prayer knelt; when the western wing
was added, one vast sigh
arose & made its way into the earless sky.
Lifts were installed, many had their ashes hauled.
Parents in the throng looked down appalled,

In the end the mighty roof was hoisted on.
The event transpired throughout the city at dawn,
foot upon violent foot
converged to shining Henry in the risen sun,
question tormented the multitude one by one
to see to what use it would now be put.

DEATH all endeth, Henry to Sybil saith.
Sybil regurgitates, no word from her.
Ah, ah, no word from her.
Flashing existence seems from her to incur
a bitter silence, vomit, assent to his death
black as it must occur.

Black black black but not at the beginning
which was when? Ha ha we never remember.
And in the end we won't.
Suppose we wake up then a shrivelled cunt:
we won't.
At that point too Fall will turn into December.

December: the noblest. After the pains & glories of the Fall
dead winter: snow car-high, snow shoulder-high,
snow cinema-high:
hope shoulder-high for death:
no word from her at all.
Death all endeth, Henry to Sybil saith.

Jan 68

HENRY scampered, young. Henry doddered old.
Steps bothered him. Packages in both hands
unbothered him.
His figure altered not, he remained slim
but the memory loss. Persons from other lands
read him their poems bold,

demure, in Chinese, Bengali, Spanish, and chanted
in high Cambodian. Henry was enchanted
on an Iowa afternoon
but what did it have to do with his failing life,
his whisky curse, his problems with his wife,
when 'Let's have a new tune'

said Haydn to somebody? He brought his troubles home
and they were grand, and foreign poetry
was foreign poetry;
valiant, but not as brilliant as a comb
to make him less dishevelled. Old Henry never wept
but then he never slept.

Jan 68

Its source obscure, the river make its way
all the same seaward, and animals can't count,
puzzling Henry.
Some insects can, and birds, and the amount
of organisms is over a million, say
the author of these books driving Henry crazy

with their zooids & their interfascicular cambium.
Did he after all take the wrong courses?
How can a man be so ignorant & live?
He dodged his way in & out of his resources
which he'd thought many, but numb
& structured like a sieve

he addressed hisself to a problem more complex
(the starter won't start, his lecture will be late)
: will she or won't she come?
If not, why so? And *if* so, will we sex?
Questions more vexed, absolutely innate,
worse than their damned interfascicular cambium.

20 Feb 68

13

Long (my dear) ago, when rosaries
based Henry's vaulting thought, at seven & six,
Henry perceived in the sky
your form amidst his stars. He fought to please
you & God daily. Seldom wicked tricks
surfaced into his I.

Malice remained, in this man, moribund
unto this hour and even at this hour
it's sleepy & can't bother.
Let demons do. But evils other conned
Henry sufficiently to blot or sour
your forms & the form of Father.

I was *the* altar-boy he depended on
on freezing twilit mornings, after good dreams.
Since when my dreams have changed.
Could Father wrong occurred to Henry gone
fearful, grown. Out of the world of seems
our death has us estranged.

20/21 Feb 68 (second) 1:50 a.m.

14

So and só tired I cannot cast a shadow.
It's Bellevue or the Tombs if I'm found out.
How have I come so far?
Exploited Henry passed his avatar.
Unrecognizable Henry hurled a shout
round the mirrors on the meadow.

His friend wrote on incomprehensibly,
the Viet war hottened up horribly,
Nixon is back in sight.
Shall willing Henry study art history
or Number or write letters or test the text
of *The Merry Wives* tonight?

Harmless his present thought as Ross's in
The Right and The Good: but is his discipline
necessary?
The mirrored meadow called all relative,
he'll take his baby to the circus, he'll live,
'A drink, no thank you, sorry.'

1 Mar 68

This most young gifted girl, antic, self-slain
Henry's protégée, on Monday morning,
in her parents' basement—
a letter long & desperate she sent
to Henry Sunday
arriving in the same mail with her death

saving his answering—shovels, the sound
of clods on a coffin, a fortnight underground
wandring shuddering thro' the air
goes *her* soul? or is it vanisht all
two thousand miles off, inaccessible
to Henry in his despair?

Some meeting of the minds can we imagine
once she is used to it? I'm used to it,
day by distracting day.
I expect her welcome when I follow her
to God's sad afterthought, Catholics both
but Henry won't take that way.

Unprotected, Henry took off east
& west, and he is willing to make new friends
& God knows they welcome *him*.
but somehow there's no one to talk with, like Timon's feast,
somehow in this town of 9,000 souls with their ends
they have gone to their means, dull as a hymn,

leaving Henry solo, honey,
to that terrible booze bruising his future, dear,
solo, with accurate money
& a brain, a brain, that should have left him clear
years ago, honey, of this *stuff* he drinks
& of every damned thing he thinks.

Business conversation fills the bar
Coleridge with his problems fades
I have never forgiven Empson for one remark
about ebullient Henry's ebullience.
Henry was only lookin fer a place to park,
Mr Coleridge, for decades.

Skidmore Fête

FIFTEEN young ladies sang out Henry's Songs
three hours, and Cookie Palmer sang the best.
Seventy-five young ladies
listened, rapt. How many of Henry's wrongs
would have seemed righted, there, had he been there
to listen, say on his knees

in a far corner, unknown, the second man,
Mr Nightingale being first, the coach, the prime
of the delicate occasion,
rehearsed for a month! O Henry in his time
might have been amused by the girls' voices
while Cookie Palmer rejoices

over 46, 15 and 60, pal,
God knows what they're about, but I can swear
they're not worth her attention,
Cookie's I mean, I think I mean at all
any of theirs, any of all their care
with the drinking & the tension.

Henry, conceited & unscrupulous,
complacent in his royalty, lit a fresh cigar
and lookt about him.
Everything beckoned to him,—as not to us,—
whether for need of relief, or for who he are,
& for why the light is so dim.

Why is there any light? he wondered, rich
with himself, yes, & a fraction of a snarl
escaped developing Henry.
Sermons came thro', in English, to his niche.
Wings went by, feathery, & in marble.
He took a deep breath, he,

and held it until his history was known.
'Love,' he let it out, & puffed. 'The world's' he said
'pale yellow & dark blue.'
So saying, he ascended toward his throne
whence would flow solace for really the world's blood-red
and Henry knows that too.

2 Mar 68

'The sovereign I,' called Henry yet again
in storm & weariness, and 'No,' said she,
'We are not that way made,
we check & balance on a dancing deck,
brutes & angels, & too there are men—'
That is not all she said

but all I heard, in my condition, blind
with weather, whether, & all them great things,
sane trios Mozart heard,
Freud & John Marshall made explicit, kind,
not quite inflexible with broken wings
to fly like a wing'd bird

not quite to peace. A voice came from the bench:
'When the focus is on the particular acts of one branch,
it is not difficult to conjure
the parade of horrors
which can flow from unreviewable power,'
so Henry warned his hearers.

JUDGE WARREN E. BURGER, IN THE POWELL CASE, 1968

14 Mar 68

Who was now one branch, who was now another,
& now a third: sometimes they sing together
but mostly (they confess) not.
The harmony lies also in the hear
of the persuaded, yielding engineer
who lets the damned train rot

outside the terminal or coxes it home,
greetings like shouts of joy, meetings like a moan
await this journey's end.
The song was made in darkness, to be set alit
(obstacles placed by the singer in the way of it)
by a hearer like a new friend.

Gravid Henry groaning, tousled like a mop—
these labour-pains, how can he keep it up?
Is it our need he feels,
or something just between the two of them,
Henry & the English language, his stratagem
besides the banana peels.

14 Mar 68

Tennis in Middle Age

I DOUBLE-FAULT, I double-fault, I double-
fault. Oyez, my wife can serve in court
& I cream her serves.
She wins, ever Henry slumps. I hurt
with all this losing & the universal rubble
& the absence of her curves.

To be continually beaten by somebody absolutely no good!
O Ellsworth Vines, & Allison Danzig,
& the subtle Perry
who threw his racket down in rage at the failure of a smash
at Forest Hills, where Henry was a member
in the semi-finals, with Johnny Hope Doeg,

the big serve, something rather less in the rest of his game,
no resource like Parker's backhand, the Australian bit,
I ballboyed for Helen Wills Moody, I pines,
Agutter my coach was rallying with her. What is fame?
A lifetime's working trips you over it.
O Ellsworth Vines!

20 May 68

With arms outflung the clock announced: Ten-twenty.
Dozens of demons sprang & preyed on Henry.
All on a heavy morning.
The baby was ill, the sky was dark, the I
was Id, somebody put the sky on like a lid,
somebody who is not returning.

Oh we'll wait. After all, after all.
The Doubter & the rest. They rested all,
on the night of the crucifying.
Perhaps their dreams were something truly remarkable.
Perhaps their dreams had what to do with his dying—
but that was very lonely.

Haldol & Serax, phenobarbital,
Vivactil, by day; by deep night Tuinal
& Thorazine,
kept Henry going, like a natural man.
I'm waiting for them to work, as sometimes they can,
honey, in the bloodstream.

June 68

Good words & irreplaceable: serenade, schadenfreude,
angst & malheur, we need them, we bow to them:
what raving genius
in our past coined such wisdom? I cannot know.
Nor can you, my deep dear. You cannot know.
They were ineffable.

Who coined despair? I hope you never hear,
my lovely dear, of any such goddamned thing.
Set it up on a post
and ax the post down while the angels sing,
& bury the stenchful body loud & clear
with an appropriate toast.

Who made you up? That was a thin disguise:
the soul shows through. You are my honey dear.
Come, come & live with me.
I can deal with everything but your eyes
in tears—tears I invented & put there,
during our mystery.

24 June 68

An Afternoon Visit

DEEP she sank into Henry's mind, such years ago.
Now with her children & her lawyer-husband O
she is visited by Henry.
Burned she his gorgeous letters: he kept hers:
some assistant professor for the curious
& to become an associate

will utter with footnotes them, so all can read
& wonder at her spirit, tumultuous
as if a spirit could bleed,
now comes the visit mild & decorous
with Henry's child, & this will happen again
in the world of women & men.

A Henry James title. —Spare her, Mr Bones.
Preserve her the privacy which she now owns. —
—O yes, I will, I will.
After our deaths, then will the problem rise
when my blind eyes look into her blind eyes,
in the bronze damp & the chill.

25 June 68

SHE blest his states. However, he interfered
largely with her life, in the future, & beyond
her current life.
Drest in a handsome print, short short short weird,
she gave him drinks & he became quite fond
again of her, next to his wife.

She destroyed his letters: that he held against her.
O but he loved her & he loved her still.
To sink into that abyss
might be a triumph. Inconceivable.
She comes to me with her past & present a blur.
Fancy now, darling, this:

Another I, another you, long since
planned together our lives, and in the future
we will do so again.
Your colour is a joy. Your hues & tints—
ravening thro' the world—disgrace nature,
and we will do better then.

25 June '68, aft.

26

OLD codger Henry contain within hisself
Henry young, Henry almost beautiful
Henry the seducer
Henry the mad young artist, with *no* interest in pelf
whereas now he takes steps to keep both his bank accounts full
just like: you, Sir!

Henry could never put up with litter.
Litter grew on him as he grew, until
you couldn't see his tables
for the damned *litter* of papers, glasses,
visible incoherences—& so was the floor, pal;
Henry lived like something from Aesop's Fables.

Codger Henry, desperatingly tired,
nevertheless got *fed up* with this state
which alas only he could fix.
I draw the veil over whom then he hired
but I promise they did not solve his fate.
He bared his rare watch. *It* ticks.

4 July 68, 7:15 a.m.

27

At this point in time, millions of souls collect
to say McTeague's gilt tooth should not have been taken away
& other American tragedies
imaginary & real: Hart Crane in Paris, wreckt,
Adlai in London, looking on a day
for a terrible partner, a tease.

O yes, at this point in time the American soul
gathers its forces for the good of man
but it has memories.
Henry Adams denied this, & he was right
but for the few the place is crawling with ghosts
like lice in a pan.

When will the fire be turned on? and by whom?
heating the memory & soul alike
until both crisp.
Not soon, I wonder, but in some lead-shielded room
mistakes are being made like the Third Reich
perhaps, I lisp.

8:22 a.m., 4 July 68

We Were in the 8th Grade

QUIET his loves lay, at   the bottom of his mind.
Now & then, O now & then, at intervals,
he took one out & inspected it.
Like a clown, or a dog trainer, or a strong kind
of man, he placed it under the waterfalls
& expected it to submit.

They did him homage. Which he did repay
with memory. One in the end wrote to him,
saying are you the same one?
He was the same one, & she published his un-
book, long since lost, about a trip to Neptune
in two volumes, let's say,

in hard brown paper, in her Spenserian hand,
with the title (forgotten) & his then name
& the important date.
O she was a golden one, higher than Henry
by a head, called Helen Justice, and
then, until now, she disappeared.

7 July 68

Cover up—Don't tell all—are our laws too.
Henry a hundred times, to his chagrin,
understated the bad case.
Blessings on the Henry ever a megrim,
peace to the warring dynasties, black is blue
I blindly swear. My face

is red, pal, from my many many faults.
It seems to seem a master of Tolstoy's starts & halts,
chill reality.
Hurt lay the fallen child in the August barn
we say 'Well, next time it will be our turn,'
but that is not so for Henry.

A thousand thousand disasters he escapt.
His hand against his forehead
in such ways out he scraped
Svelte lay the marina & we took the boat
at 40 miles an hour to a secret coast
of an old building where we were fed.

after July 29, 1968

3:30 of a Thursday afternoon
in August, when little girls needs cakes,
my ladies are asleep:
my wife, my protégée (an affair with a coon),
I'm reading the Q of *Much Ado* for its own sakes,
I find I made notes to keep.

I find I made notes to keep, on my dear ladies,
my daughter & the summer afternoon,
& the whole corpus of Shakespeare,
my wife just said 'NO' to the baby, never mind Please,
'And when I say no I mean no' — 'See my ice-cream cone'
five seconds later.

He thought and a star danced, Beatrice was born,
not of his best but very good. Othello welled up,
terrible for fear
in his mind also full of women forlorn—
All's Well—his orchard, a summer afternoon,
                              Desdemona came to a stop
in the imagination of Shakespeare.

Henry's Fate

ALL projects failed, in the August afternoon
he lay & cursed himself & cursed his lot
like Housman's lad forsooth.
A breeze sometimes came by. His sunburn itcht.
His wife was out on errands. He sighed & scratcht.
The little girls were fiddling with the telephone.

They wanted candy, the which he gave them.
His entire soul contorted with the phlegm.
The sun burned down.
Photos of him in despair flooded the town
or city. Mourned his many friends, or so.
The little girls were fiddling with the piano.

He crusht a cigarette out. Crusht him out
surprising God, at last, in a wink of time.
His soul was forwarded.
Adressat unbekannt. The little girls with a shout
welcomed the dazzling package. In official rime
the official verdict was: dead.

August 68

SINEWY Henry let his ladies hang
down from his arms, in arabesques, whilst he
sought formulas for them.
Great was his physical pain, he grimly sang,
at many points, but others' agony
was greater still. A stratagem

surfaced: O let them all be married off,
but two would not. In mental pain he dared
anyone, under the sky.
Some slid away & children had. Enough!
he cried, I have grief more than I have shared,
into the innocent eye.

Long lost sight of, the two & Henry danced
in a London masquerade. He took a rook,
and that was good for his side.
His brain was pierced, at which the others glanced.
Sat Henry's lady down with Henry's book,
Henry's sorrow & pride.

3 Nov 68

A MAN stood up from gross affliction, stood
trembling, in a marsh. Whither would he go?
The land-birds were clamorous.
He couldn't read his maps. His staff of wood
sank in everywhere. He fancied on him below
were clustered the wraths of us.

And I won't call him wrong. We hated him
for all that dismal & the tufts of spirit.
—Mr Bones, they repents.
Quiet you. —I am elected to create a hymn
in classical Chinese, which we inherit,
dense with abundant sense

to the few who for him were against the mob.
Hao I start, *jen* I continue. Cries
from terns & jays, midst papyri,
point out my message, which is my last job.
The world has ended, to no one's surprise.
We won't return him to I.

3 Nov 68

LEAVES are in heaps, snow flies, I wear a hat,
and it is all but a year since you made your bid,
your final one, since sixteen
saw your deficient first, the ski-hose that
wrinkling your brow you doused with lighter-fluid
& set fire to.

I bore my birth. What more do I have to bear?
She took up knives & scratched up her left arm
hideous to behold.
She wore ungainly sweaters. She took no care
of her fine appearance: sloppy came to harm
in the big basement.

Her mother was in the kitchen after breakfast. Why,
Rita went downstairs, where the jukebox & the guns were.
She used to hit the punching-bag
in hospital gloveless till her knuckles were bloody,
calling my name with each blow. Her mother runs
at the shout, but then there's a shot.

12 Nov 68

Apollo 8

BIZARRE Apollo, half what Henry dreamed,
half real, wandered back on stage from the other wing
with its incredible circuitry.
All went well. The moon? What the shadow seemed
to Henry in his basement: shadows gathering
around an archaic sea

with craters grand on the television screen,
as dead as Delphi treeless, tourist gone
& the god decidedly gone.
Selene slid by the Far-Shooter, mean
of plagues & arrows, whom the doom clampt on,
both embarrassed in the Christian dawn.

(That roar you hear as the rocket lifts is money, hurt.)

Which dawn has ended, and it is full day.
And the mountain of Mao flesh, did it once respond
'Let all moons bloom'? O no,
these events are for kids & selenographers, say,
a deep breath, creating no permanent bond
between the passive watchers & moonglow.

THE New Year? Henry sank back on his haunches.
It certainly could not be denied that the old year was ashes,
ashes, all fall down.
He shopped until he bled, all the way downtown.
He constructed lists of his surviving friends
and of the others the ends.

Toward the close, heavy snow helped to blanket his thought,
no one dead or alive was anywhere
going, every battle was fought.
Mary-Mary at the January sales
would represent him, contrary. The mails
will lessen. Lectures by the pair

grimly will begin, with Epictetus,
parties will thud to a finish, the tree'll come down
& shedding out & over.
Who shall we say was the heroine of Christmas
but Henry's lady & the little baby. Clown
Henry, lying above her.

23 Dec 68

GLISTENING, Henry freed himself from money
by making enough.
Not much, enough.
His bills in Hell will easy be to pay,
no laundry there,
no long-distance telephone.

No bars. Instead he'll have to render up
every drink ever he had.
O that would not be good, that would be bad.
Hell *is* said to be bad,
but worse than earth? I can't believe that, I stop.
If I don't churn my legs, I drop.

Drop all the same, in the end, cried fatal Henry
whose solo love was giant Sophocles
in his heights & final peak
of weirdness & blood, like the mysteries of the sea
and which let us forgive, like mysteries:
I do lie down here, meek.

HENRY PUSSY-CAT

An eye-opener, a nightcap, so it goes.
One for the road, eight to pass out, so it goes.
So it goes.
They say if the Harvard Provision Co. shut down
there wd be no more excellent teaching in that town.
Full professors wd come to blows.

Too much can hardly be made of the eccentric view
that sees liquor in quantity as a sedative
& for poets dissociative.
I won't linger over that. That's up to you.
Like the 3 kinds of marijuana I was recently offered
in Illinois, like a bird

of passage, bard of passage, oh well I
somehow refused them all & got home safe.
Also a 'sexy' fat woman
was offered me, whom likewise I refused, I
with my intent to be true beyond belief,
which is merely human.

THE assault on immortality begins.
Put your rimes in order, marshal your thoughts,
give it all a jump.
Translation will cast the whole thing down, like bins.
They've tried it in Polish, Italian, German, lots,
& it all came out a lump.

Henry's thought, in Henry's original words—
although it would not win the Nobel Prize—
was the point.
Let Icelanders & Latin Americans have it, for the birds.
They never crowned Ibsen or Frost. I open my eyes
wide. Let's wreck the joint,

assuming sea & air, to pass to there.
The Swedes are all up in their formal costumes,
ignorant of Chinese.
Ignorant of English (American version). Hair
down all my girl's smooth nape menaces tombs
& bids me lie at ease.

? May 69

Rembrandt van Rijn obit 8 October 1669

—It's 300 years, Mr Bones, since the great one died.
Can you find it in your soul to make a word
or have you forgotten how?
—Sting me, you reptile, but let the Self-imaginer lie.
They took his house, they took all his armor, absurd,
he lives in furnisht rooms now.

The Biblical figures come, they come & go,
his children mostly are dead, & Saskia,
his mode has disappeared.
He workt on the 100 plates like a soul below,
a man who never did a wrong thing, like Bix's jazz,
was he of the end affeared.

Over & over. Flashing lights, deep glooms.
The natural soul performing, as it will,
if you have the mind & fingers.
A gazelle is flying from a lion. Furnisht rooms
in filthy Amsterdam, where he lay ill.
His making world-wide lingers.

1 Oct '69

Hallowe'en

THIS Hallowe'en goes out my baby then
for tricks or treats alone: I dump here
dealing out treats.
She's almost seven. She insisted. Alone.
Two or three other little girls climb with her.
That's the end of our feats

when we scrambled, father & daughter, up long steps,
Daddy lagging behind. Beautiful, she got many.
Her costumes was superb.
This is the end of Daddy, the shallowing of the depths
of her childhood, when bearded Daddy was any.
Daddy, parked at the curb,

will watch his baby, muttering in Latin,
scrambling up the steps of Smith or Vassar saying
'I want a Yale man with a yacht
after my degrees, whereon, me in satin,
my Daddy can spend his last years without paying,
revising his works or not.'

1969

HE sits in the dawn, if it can be called dawn,
of midwinter in Minnesota, scribbling.
The dog prowls & whimpers,
being in heat. His human ladies are asleep,
the baby & her mother. His lamp is on,
another overcast.

Where hide the brilliances whereof he dreamed
in swift youth, loud, unable to recite
the actual history of disappointment
that would be his, and that would be all right.
Two of his books are being put into German,
one was earlier in Polish.

So here failed Henry sits, counting his losses,
not wholly in despair, and growing hungry.
He slept longer than usual:
one cliff he had to descend, clinging to mosses,
woke him though. I would call him half-angry,
an object of wintry pity.

TAKE that, old clown, & that & that & that,
who roost among my trousers:
at 65 do you plan to be browsers
among the young'uns? Let the young'uns have it.
Closer settled the sky, in rain not snow,
it's odd though,

odd the distance frantic between father & son, between the
                                        son & the father
who would have pickt him up & kissed him rather
but felt he had to die
so he went outside with a gun, gracefully.
I receive this information, I.

It's humanhood kept some of them along,
old pal, and I would not put that down.
Wind it up with a sorry song.
In a worthier end I'd meet you all downtown
and we'd have a ball, but that would be the end,
toward which we all depend.

GREAT flaming God, bend to my troubles, dear.
I am asked to give up a way of life
established 22 years ago,
and by my dear wife, in anxiety & fear.
My greatest efforts may not be enough.
My thought ceases to flow

forward to drinks & cigarettes & such
and sticks in the now. Where I must be
for years, for years, for years.
I am not myself, it suddenly appears,
but horrible habits, habits, habits, much
like those we ghastly see

in tragic drama—but the hero dies.
Henry survives his holocaust. Walk on!
with your retching cough
& burning tongue & your sobrieties
in the Fifth Act, to bid the soldiers moan
and shoot. Applause sounds, off.

I'M reading my book backward. It sounds odd.
It came twenty minutes ago. The hell with god.
A student just called up
about a grade earlier in the year.
The hell with students. And my mother ('Mir')
did the indexes to this book.

There's madness in the book. And sanenesses,
he argued. Ha! It's all a matter of
control (& so forth) of the subject.
The subject? Henry House & his troubles, yes
with his wife & mother & baby, yes
we're now at the end, enough.

A human personality, that's impossible.
The lines of nature & of will, that's impossible.
I give the whole thing up.
Only there resides a living voice
which if we can make we make it out of choice
not giving the whole thing up.

A Nerve Is Pinched

AFTER some weeks in hospital he
(the main doctor—Henry's psychiatrist—
also looked in)
initiated the word 'damaged' & also *'crushed.'*
This was an immense relief to Henry
who had past 'pinched' suffering been.

Between two vertebrae, in a muscle spasm,
they conjecture, the greater occipital nerve
had hell,
the whole left side of Dr brain a holocaust
and numb its scalp.

Hot-packs, deep massage, and TRACTION
of the neck—jumbling of rocks in the top of the skull.
A few months of, maybe he will be well.
Masada saw a bloody serious action
against the alternatives, Roman slavery.
All killed themselves.

II

Sherry, & X Overseas

THEY had in common O & rum-&-Coke
(hers) & blackberry brandy (shudder, his)
& a sullen selfhood; and no more O.
She sought a how to put the message O
that what had not been might gnash to its end.

She came to me to sing upon this theme,
but a sorry declarative sentence was all my do.
No altitude! no depth of loss! Only
a vexed impulse of half-contempt despite
my fondness toward her strong that this one hope

in all her all but thirty years that this
the surfaced thing should fizzle.
Daughter, it was not yours: of whom I've seen
only truly to *love* one spasm of courage.
Your living must alter, nightly I pray.
Apathy toward Limbo

volcanic made this once, of which you said
afterward you felt silly: ah you were wrong,
awarding your being nothing, as usual.
I'll dare my utter all for you. For me.

Our Lord descend again on you, I at first light wish
& now at 3 a.m. sober I beg.
My dear, you too must bow down, unthinkable stance,
& give up, & summon to you blindly trust, & pray.
He always hears. Even I, in my degree,
hear what you cannot say.

BEING a dog & being treated like one
except by Congress & the President's wife
Being also a cat & being treated like one
petted, purred at & feared

I can't say who I am. I hang on to Catullus' love for his dead
                                                      brother,
I love my living one, & there is art
there is (scholarship) the finding of things out
there is my wife & baby daughter.

'I'm not a baby: I'm a li'l girl,'
she began two years ago to growl at me.
'Darling,' I said, 'you will always be my baby.
As you stumble up the steps of Smith or Vassar

grumbling in Latin, you will be *my baby*.

I'm afraid you'll fracture hearts, in New Haven & Cambridge,
with your natural wit & your built-in beauty
got (darling) from your mother. So: take it easy.
Let them proffer their best. But: do *your* best.

Say nothing but politenesses. Try them out, give them a chance,
in company & alone.'
The lady President of Smith's final advice to her graduating
                                                      class:
'And, girls, keep your legs together.'

May my beloved friend, your godfather Robert Fitzgerald
from his eminence at Harvard & Ithaca
often pray for you. And may you live long
& sometimes visit my grave.

Martha is a silly waffle. It is Easter morning.
I am trying from 55 to convince her 7
Christ left the tomb or the nameless Hebrew grave
& appeared to Peter.

Her teeth are in good order, two gone, which we paid money
for.
So: I can't say it's like extracting a tooth.
Some other metaphor. I don't find one.
She *barely* believes me.

I hope her faith will increase until the Fourth Gospel
will be at her pretty teen-aged fingertips.
But let her skepticism live also
amiable like lambs with her faith.

My doubts fight my faith.

The Presence

Turn around. Did you hear that? Did you see that?
Do I hover in your room, for this first time?
I can't *touch* you, but otherwise am I welcome
to sniff & see my fill?

I can't speak back, but will you talk to me
secretly & in tears of *anything?*
Take me as of your lonesome soul a function
& make me ache with you?

What pamphlet's that you're frowning over?
What quirk of actual joy have you recalled today?
What keeps you sorriest in all your past?
What most, if you could have it, do you want?

Unopened letters on your writing-table
aren't they? What do you fear?
Gothic follies black against a skyline
play against you this year?

One tone made of many,
breaking & joining like the unseen water,
possesses, may be, your heart. Whisper to me
who have come upon you, after so long, at last.

Gloss, bounce: all gone. I interpret:
if crowded by private pain your face looks up
unseeing toward where I might be . . .
A saint or a fool, I wonder.

Anyway, a lot of more sweet handling:
fingertips, palms, pink tongue
lingering in & out pink.
God's angels fall down dazed for the whole world to look at.

Enlightening Morning

A MERCILESS, sad letter from a 'teen,
who heard me talk in Golden Valley.
'Your blindness amazes me.' 'I'm the one you asked
with wry wit whether I was a boy or a girl.'

'I have to admire your total control over any self-doubt.'
'Oh, something else I admire, your ability to lie.'
'Can you remember, now, what it's like to be young?
I often wonder if it will ever be over.'

A strange, rare insight: it was never over
because it never began: childhood imploded
at twelve & was succeeded by nineteen,
not young at all. I've not been where this girl is,

stark-naked, insolent & miserable.
From when at last I came to, I was armed,
noblesse oblige, & halfway to command—
to her she says I seem 'an oddity . . .

a dinosaur'—to me she looms knee-high
an entirely new form of pathetic carnivore.

Roots

YOUNG men (young women) ask about my 'roots,'—
as if I were a *plant*. Yeats said to me,
with some pretentiousness, I felt even then,
'London is useful, but I always go back

to Ireland, where my roots are.' Mr Eliot,
too, worried about his roots
whether beside the uncontrollable river
the Mississippi, or the Thames, or elsewhere.

I can't see it. Many are wanderers,
both Lawrences, Byron, & the better for it.
Many stay home forever: Hardy: fine.
Bother these bastards with their preconceptions.

The hell with it. Whether to go or stay
be Fate's, or mine, no matter.
Exile is in our time like blood. Depend on
interior journeys taken anywhere.

I'd rather live in Venice or Kyoto,
except for the languages, but
O really I don't care where I live or have lived.
Wherever I am, young Sir, my wits about me,

memory blazing, I'll cope & make do.

Mpls, Mother

I

'At least one temple for the city's tutelary god'—
seems a small thing to ask. But the building here
of interest was put up the other day by a Japanese
to enclose some Upper Midwest insurance men.

II

Surely *some* emotion will be appropriate?
A Dubliner who came ten days ago
to feast in one of our colleges a year
says he's written already a poem called you.

III

I've lived here off & on for sixteen years
and can't tell if—inspired at last by him—
I bend my art to it
whether to deplore or celebrate your essential nonentity.

IV

Site without history! City of *lakes*, it's true,
but only the Lake of the Isles possesses distinction
and that's contaminated for swimming and
the boating's trivial, a few canoes.

V

Size? Ah, but L.A., a sort of sub-continent,
ranks only as 'six suburbs in search of a city,'
unified solely by smog & unspeakable freeways.
Where, Mother of Hennepin, shall I seek *your* center?

VI

And who, I enquire in vain
at the corner of Fifth & Hennepin, was Hennepin?
Professor Toynbee speaks of 'the rudiments of a soul'
that you must have evolved in order to become a 'city.'

VII

Where here then is Dionysus venerated,
inspirer of poets?—for you have had poets:
Mr Tate, retired now & back in his South,
this impetuous young mick, & your humble inhabitant.

VIII

What martyr's cry quickens our civil blood,
Wolfe Tone's, Parnell's? Whose sacrifice
on a *noche triste* centuries alive
enables an ultimate homogeneity?

IX

Heavily, heavily Scandinavian,
your proper only feast an old Swede one
I forget too, your touted waterfall
flowing but by appointment, on a budget.

X

Vast eyesore granaries, pathetic monopoly newspapers,
a pretty little Mall we're so vain of,
the redman in the gutter, a University
only by the voters of our own State hated.

XI

Even on *this* continent, I prefer Mexico D.F.,
& Ciñti Ohio, so near above turfy Kentucky,
& suddenly since World War II unrecognizable & unbearable
                                    New York,
home of sharp elbows short tempers & Puerto Ricans.

XII

O leafing these volumes thro' without surprising
one uttered word worth my preserving here
(*Carthago delenda est, No pasarán*)
or sentiment seeming intimately yours,
I fall almost to despair,

XIII

Place of great winds and higher & higher drifts
far into March, I recognize you by your frozen waters
& fur-capped denizens helping each other out,
grinning, with stuck cars.

> [*The following stanza, in longhand and unnumbered, was
> attached to the typescript for inclusion in the poem.*]

You warned me, dear, to increase underwear
When I moved here, and hell I haven't done it.
It's true I often pass in hospital
the good bit of the year.

Che

I MAKE a connexion: in your death & life
I see the Third Temptation overcome,—
foreseen (which bulks out as   remarkable enough
for poor men rarely aimed) and overcome;

so I'll pretend I'm you thro' certain lines
and maybe I'll improve. You can't object,
you are Bolivian molecules, dim slime
so far as judgment comes, it's ruined years now

and many across our world sweating to 'read' you,
over some slobs of which I claim advantage
as sequent: Sticking to your goddamn word
I couldn't care less except to save myself.

So saying, I burn myself out of my way.

I wonder where rich Mother fetched her blood—
from Aragon or Huelva?—obstinate,
proud to all hurrying deaths, seductive, amusing,
reckless as a pampas fire, follow-the-leader . . .

Fuck my dry father's, you wind up with me
breathless, fighting for breath,
sucking from dipped chalk ink (said to be fatal),
seeking out companionable lepers up the Amazon.

O vampire bats with rabies, bite not me,
I'm not that brave. We enjoy less & less
tortoise feet daily with the toenails off,
incredible rapids & loud jaguars.

You sought it all for pure joy, anyway,
sacrifices, the bit. I'm screwed if I'll praise you;
enjoy and fear you; you open a hope
we're not contemptible necessity.

No, Matthew 4:10 was the point & the only point:
to head for what but fearlessness and love,
anything less or other become the Devil himself
to suck the ample anus of, & sign in:

'Lost soul. Sold, for something less
than man.' From *Siempre*, a gross U.S. map
all mouthing faces, all but a baffled Chief
and sorry yippee, with mouths drawn down shut.

Begin with shame. The woman or man not revolutionary
isn't. Where he found 'no will to fight,
leaders corrupt,' he went Elsewhere,—
versatile as the word 'set' & as single.

Stuck with a message. Stuck, worse, with a witness.

'You plebeian Don Juan'

Sentimental inflation & brutal precipitancy
marked months his course with women. Oh, he lied;
but he believed his lies, and careful girls
grew silly swiftly as cream-puffs & burned.

Six at a time, or so, built he fires under,
no trouble too great for his gourmandizing,
savouring their frantic inflamed epistles
long after he had ceased to answer them.

When one would flag, a postcard quickened back
to feverish endeavours & ill-health
her natural embers,—graphed by him with rich
warm self-embracements by her terrible heat.

I

TEN summers past, a continent away
we were élève & Maître, poet & actress,
now what is this a thousand miles apart
       (my dear) midsummer madness?

Solicitude & admiration gone
wild in a moment, at this end, and you
write just as wild immediately back
       (my dear) with fever too!

I think, I think I mistook a passion of sympathy
violently put for somehow lust
and met it without reflexion in mid-air
       (my dear) suddenly *with* lust.

However that just was, between us suddenly
feeling is streaming, covers are thrown back
on a bottom sheet that's burning white at your place
       (my dear) for my   travel & attack.

II

Only I've got to go a long long way first
in the opposite direction with dismay
and now on paper ink to say
       if your thirst equals my thirst,

65

if weeks away your bed will still be waiting
as O your letter yesterday not quite
but almost all confesses, turned-back & bright
        for our September meeting.

We're going to need high faith & fantastic will
to cross alive this desert of time to come,
hours & days & 'planes & cities & some
        unnerving doubt, until

the distant countries telescope & close
down into your mouth in an airport & your eyes
open on mine there where probably will arise
        what yesterday to your letter arose.

Loss

IMMEASURABLY sad, O long ago
she ceased her being with mine, mine like a fuse
sputtering toward a common doom.
She said in her heart 'I must create my own.'
I learn this now on a mild & terrible morning.

Too late—too far distrust & guilt & pain
too late for any return or any beginning
of any nearness or hope again.
All desire's blown out of me by loss,
an aching backward only, dull, of our marvellous love.

III Fragments and Unfinished Poems

Oedipus the King (OPENING)

OEDIPUS: Old Cadmus' sons: why   throng you me these
                                            sieges
         with imploring branches while the city too
         burns incense and at once paeans & wails?
         Distrusting messengers, my children, I,
         I myself, all-famous Oedipus,
         am come. Now, aged sir, fitting to speak
         for these, say in what mood you stand,
         afraid or solemnly questing: since I will
         all your assistance: I were a clod else.

PRIEST: O Oedipus, who rules, see us indeed
         before thine altars, of all ages, some
         fledglings, others old, I the priest of Zeus,
         some chosen by the young, but all the people more
         with branches, in the markets sit, & at both shrines
         of Pallas & besides Ismenus' ashes.
         For the city, as you see, tosses & groans,
         nor from the bloody surge can lift her head,
         ripened but blighted corn, blighted the wombs,
         the plague of fire, come down, ravages us,
         emptying Cadmus' house to fill rich Hell.

THE DEPRECATION *but*

My dear little devil
            whom I do not love
'Granada's wine? Their grapes haven't suffered enough.'
Perhaps I am not ready—certainly have no right—
to palate your essence or your accidents;
allow me, though, a certain alacrity of the Curious.

As in the zoo *only*, except for my guinea pigs
& depthless Rufus, I confront animals,
having so much to learn of them & myself!,
so sole from *paper* does my vision mount
vertiginous & untriangulated you.

Your daily & your holidaily both
I'd more by more & more intensely take in;
so let me by return. Over all there's
this need to watch your Time—my watch won't do

(Why? well, it's geometric optics, where
perception is a kind of problem-solving,
a *betting* on the most probable interpretation of sensory data,—
dangerous in that we must adapt to what we have created:

the danger that of creating a world
beyond the restraints of our intelligence:
a world we cannot see.) Over-going you! :—:
Henry Moore's great sundial in Printing House Square!

All the same, somehow I *know* enough of you!
Thanks for the troops: they were delicious!

How can I *scale* letters you will not write?
You are withholding information! dear.
I can't be sure a crime has been committed.
My enquiry is at a standstill.

                    your character brewing your conduct

is a definite & durable 'something'
I have to try & measure, though measurement
may yield me only, abstract, unreal, a North Pole
or a line of longitude upon a map.

Be farther off! Damn your pores!
I'll be your scientist but I paint too,
my feel for you is formal & contemplative
as well as quotidian & experimental.

Clear out your brain, & sudden for me set down
the first damned thing that flies into it, honey.
But also, then, after long thought say
what sort of impassioned person you imagine

your person in your place at that present to be.
O yes it's hard, you won't get it right
& too I'll fail to see it.
But what kiss ever in lip-history
was taken for exactly what was given?

Strange islands where in amber light float
quite without will from one pose to another . .
our letters come toward *la petite histoire*,
where love is more prominent than ideas

Washington in Love

[*4 Jan 70*]

Rectitude, & the terrible upstanding member
arms, & the broken promises of Congress
I have exercized myself to the outside
of the firing beautiful, & softness, & of
the needs of the many depending people.

Mr Jefferson thinks: with arms, in blood,
blacks will revolt
unless we form for them a separate nation

My porch is certain feet above the Potomac,
the satisfying figures

Dolley uneasy, when I pushed her hard

the softnesses of Queens, we give that up

They call me King, I confess it makes me angry

Others will come: the land's fate is upward

[*14 11. in an hour, 6 a.m., 4 Jan 70*]

I burn. She loves him. O as other men
I find I am too, and I shudder. They
are worthless to the common wealth.
David not hesitated. Why should I?
High spirits drive me on to ruin, unaccustomed.

An animal, a child, sometimes breaks my armor.
My sense of justice drawls away.

King me! I am unlike you, owing to discipline.
Hamilton is right: we must be led.

The cares of the State descended,
waking me.

Heros [*sic*] on heroes, in the years to come
I foresee a dubious one

I'm sneaking. Is it I?

My glory ebbs. I held the nation firm
against the French involvement:
I dug in.

The Union hums. Self-love is it at last,
after the Crown. Duty tells all my friends
the exception & the rule.

When every liar is your slave, when all words
garbled for hearing are your law:
what then, if justice

I wonder. The sun comes down through the   trees.
There is a strength greater than mine. I flourish
She makes me daze. A sign?

I cannot say her well. Unspeakable losses
may, for my prayer, savage her peace.

I love the French, who at the utmost stand
gave Lafayette, & I abhor their king,
but I will keep keep the country free of them

I am tempted also. Out of all these lies,
back to Mt. Vernon, where

Insult, & imputation of ill-will

[*21 beginnings*]

Mother's demands for butter, timber, money
provoked me often till I walked the floor

Intolerable Sally, loved in vain,
in secrecy, till time she married and
I told her

        whatever my merit
I could not get Dinwiddie's good opinion:
how now, as I scan back on that, was that?

I missed my father's death, in a far place.
Seasons I missed him, and no other man.
Maybe the Colonel next, who ruled me well
tumultuous & supersensitive,
faults I down long time governed, full of blood
& the craze of strong youth. Honour tortured me,
I wanted it at once, in wide applause
stainless among the welter of the rest,
shaming the slight House. My one will rode high
to its appropriate horizon: good,
for as many as may be. Out of rusted arms,
John Adams called me, and I said I'd see,
leaving the packed room. Shall I prop the state
plagued in sea-leaguered cities? Sally's sigh,
'You must be famous,' in that corridor
snaked in my soul thro' their unheard debate.

[*16 11. Sun. nt.*]

Summoned, my doubt in order, I walked back
into that fear-stiff chamber and heard out

a Boston twang, a promise, a stern plea
to my quick of obligation. He seemed long,
I said I'd ride tonight, to undertake
what might be done in Massachusetts yet,
the British gathering, the people scared,
arms few, & discipline. I bowed & left,
raging with hope. Now in my senior age,
beloved and past it, as I lounge & browse
[ADDED IN THE MARGIN:
in books I'll never finish, so I work
the flourishing plantation, my low task
remnant among my glories]
I count that instant high, when I began
to serve against our wealthy enemies
tyrannical, unfair—it made me hard,
burnished my anger to a glint of peace
in continental freedom, days of toil
out from a master vicious overseas
from ignorance.

[*33 11.? at one sitting*]

　　　　　I turned my good name in
to seek by any due means victory
in the muddle of chaos, lukewarm & afraid.
Man is a doubtful surd. I rely
in violent pride upon the fated stake
of skill to pierce me through.

I stood a healthy servant, at my time,
to the disastrous colonies. I lied,
almost, to spoil their servitude.

Wronged, in the Congress, when the French tore free
of their ancient masters, and they had helped us,
and the population of the new-born States
was all for alliance, and: Soiled in the press:

I put my arm out against treaties, risking
my standing with us. Barely I made it, costing
insufferable insult, but we did not link
our homely destiny with any State,
cherished by US or other. We stood free,

[————End?]

Here in my deep age, I do love her on,
whoever, Sally Martha, and I see
I put my strength against my loves, and I see
the steady of the nation, which is mine,
its flashing—far away will be a rival
Russia
Maybe its fleets will throng our shores.
I wish we may be dutiful. But, King,
whom Hamilton urged, and whom I would not have,
I bear my glory in a solemn peace
boring to the voters, boring to them all
They assess me cold, I do not swear
in the turmoil I'm not

I swear the heart, when will the blacks comply
into their Africa, or Southern States
alone, as Thomas Jeffers said
& Garvey

Noble. Too flexible, I doubtless wrong.
He strode his giant interests, gullible

He too much listens. Ah, but Jefferson
widely will guide them, just. Out of my hands,
the crass Republic onto him

my followers let insults fly. I hold
my solemn peace, transferring
into his hands the throne of government,
to will him well in Washington

Bitter

I cannot do it. I will not explain.
I, I am sick. They lie about me.
They reach me, and I cannot say one word
to save my reputation
I am surrounded by inferiors
I bow & am forever silent

My uniform is heavy. I don it & stand
to Stuart's orders, which he tells all over.

Who in the crazed world keeps an even peace
but Thomas Jefferson, of also Virginia.
We are divided, but the Union will
hurrah of him as I retire

[A.L.] A more complete man than I am will come.
humorous & desperate, neither of which I was.

They want me king. When Hamilton describes
necessity into another room
I making my excuses walk.

I put forth, against the French involvement, all,
and insults clubbed me home to bed.

Other revolvers, in their time, will come;
against the majority; against their elders.
Whatever my freezing joints, I wish them well.
And they will never attain to the highest posts
in the Republic, but I wish them well.

Ever since Sally, and conspicuous,
as born to be I was

I sought, I think, the Marthas of this world,
giving up Mary

The Children
Proemio

So screw you, Muses, for⠀⠀⠀⠀I have hard in my mind
a christian thing & psychosocial nuclear
environmental awful & deluded thing
—deluded by beyond 'Yea, yea,' 'Nay, nay'—
I doubt you'd even credit anyone
could credit, far less buy. But be on my side
anyway (Wonders!) whom I last invokt
for my swoln true laud of my dizzy lady
in the Princeton of New Jersey while ago
distinguished & delighting,—come over here.
You come first, Clio, so we'll chat alone
a little ere the gang throngs this fast brain
and I am up to so much I can't cherish
your feathery fingers always losing stuff
but loved for what they leave and those grave eyes
nothing forgetting if O deep enough
for long & long enough I draft at you
a fascinated passionate gaze back
wherewith we're doing business: the business is love
sole of what was/is/will, in time, and depth-read.
Okay? Now call your sister Thalia
of reprehensible invention which
wisemen still hoot at, gasping, twixt guffaws.
Soft earlobes too & round knees recommend her,
I've got to have hér with me, buy me ballpoints
when mine whites out, pat me plus-strokes when
I⠀r e a l l y⠀flag. As I am bound to, bound to

over the frightful prospect I blue toward.
We are not well informed about you ladies
frankly. Could do with data. Tough Thamyris
of violent Thrace grew suddenly very sorry
he never heard of you—cost eyes, cost voice,
that competition.

                 You, Melpomene
who take it hard since Oedipus, I won't
want you forever, but I seek your true
(far as it goes) & more dire reading of it;
so underview my project (such as it is
or proves out) in maenad trance here by me, Love.
I'll lick your eyelids, analyze your dreams,
darvon your transports, and in general
fly your fit Ariel, 'for a certain term
doomed'—till I hope for freedom back, for the air
ad lib & fare me well. You're welcome too.

Now for this topic (for the theme I *have*—
is there a second? oh, of God & men
and how they can't get on and can get on
& have to round the reservoir in peace
while the leaded atmosphere of man allows):
Just there I'm at a loss, content to be so
& verily in no hurry. But press-gang
some time, my dears, your omnicompetent
globe-trotting sisters in my mild behalf,
fully drest & more or less in my right mind,
with no date for this evening of my life.
I won't be sitting anxious for your call
exactly, but I'll answer when it comes
if it comes, meanwhile keeping out of trouble and
oiling old boots, upping to new procedures,
Tibetan exercises, meditating
Vivaldi's 'Gloria' &   two-trumpet sister-tones.
Adam's frame, I wait.

IV

Some Women in here

THE thin, flat-chested, lined lady across
stood back inside her doorway showing me breasts
little & wide-apart & cupcake-shaped
in a bitter dream I started up from just now.

They took Miss Poison off & *out* on a stretcher,
I hissed her away down the corridor.
She'd been after Big Mickey's razorblades,
the nickel mystic, the 3 a.m. blackhead bitch.

All the same, even in this same ward,
Mattie after a sob-torn talk with her long-gone grandmother
who taught her 'never to get close to them'
(they'd go away) sat flaming-faced

triumphant trust: Beautiful! I felt awe
staring across the circle at this miracle.
And butterball downtrodden Honey sprang
wild at her vile spouse after seven years!

Orbital old Annie, drunk with her wig
staggering back in, 'to telephone'
& *telephone*—when strapped under restraint
she half-smiled, wandered a little, & passed out.

I can't connect these frail, heart-qualming heroines
with solid crooks like Jon & Stack & me.
I know He does, though, and of course has plans
for the shape of our Fates more reliable than ours.

The Alcoholic in the 3rd Week
of the 3rd Treatment

HE has taught the Universe to realise itself,
and that must have been; very simple.
Surely he has a recovery for me
and that must be after all my complex struggles: *very* simple.

I do, despite my self-doubts, day by day
grow more & more but a little confident
that I will never down a whiskey again
or gin or rum or vodka, brandy or ale.

It is, after all, very very difficult to despair
while the wonder of the sun   this morning
as yesterday & probably tomorrow.
It all is, after all, very simple.

You just never drink again all each damned day.

O ALL the problems other people face
we have intensified & could not face
until at last we feel completely alone
thick in a quart of company a day.

I knew I had a problem with that stuff
& problems with my wife & child & work;
but all what help I found left me intact
safe with a quart of feral help a day.

DT's, convulsions. Hospitals galore.
Projectile vomiting hours, intravenous,
back in the nearest bar the seventh day.
God made a suggestion. I went home

and I am in the 4th week of the third treatment
& I am *hurting*, daily, & when I jerk
a few scales seem to fall away from my eyes
until with perfect clarity enough

seems to be visible to keep me sane
& sober toward the bed where I will die.
I pray that You may grant me a yielding will.

                    I pray that my will may be attuned to
                         Your will for & with me.

4th Weekend

RECOVERING Henry levelled & confronted;
helpt Mary Lou, was helpt by Mary Lou;
accepted incest, etc.
Major his insights into other burns,
grand his endeavours on their sick behalf,
on the trip into sick himself

he stuck. He did perceive a wilderness,
a need to penetrate & civilize it,
was well aware of courage
up to the effort; open to suggestions;
praying without cease; busy with his pals,
joyous in their recovery.

And that is where he stands, beloved friends.
He's opened up the roads: ended at torrents.
Toss him a hurtful clue.
He has four ah excruciated letters
(he sees) to send off. Maybe grinding them out
will bridge me back not only to those injured souls
but toward my own awful center,
finding there welcome.

The Recognition

A SCROTAL burning, night, all day, night two.
Mal-diagnosis 'infection,' ineffective treatment.
A specialist: 2nd degree burn, from friction: a cortisone
                                                    derivative.
Twenty-four hours later, not so bad!

I read her desolation, then her (worse?)
'He wants to *hurt* me too, the man I love
& have been tender & forgiving to'
and then her terrible fear before my terrible rage.

Last night on the telephone she was remote
& short, and I wondered if some awful thing
she'd had from me had come back on her
and if today she'd say 'I can't go back to it,

you'll have to leave.' Times all afternoon
this frightful verdict flickered in & out
when she came warm & worried about a *pupil*,
a little, black,—Fantastic! she still loves me!

[*Read* (1.5) is present tense.]

5th Tuesday

WE are all 44 at a fine point in this place
from 8 a.m. when Mini-group begins
until the last one the Snack Room leaves to face
another night alone where his Past grins
       saying 'This is *my* round.'

But eight of us, called the Repeaters Group,
dance on a needle of almost despair
of which the truth today is: we could hope
while we were nine, before one had to face
       out to the whiskey world.

Jack went it was, on Friday, against the word
of the staff & our word . . . violent relief
when Sunday night he & his son, absurd
in ties & jackets, for a visit brief
       looked back in, looking *good*.

We hadn't had for Jack, specially Jack
who back in treatment after just two weeks
out dry, had not budged one inch, much hope; stack
eight loving *wills* together, though, and speaks
       loudly The Group to save him.

Ticklish but trust increasing as all day
Monday no news, relaxing into *our*
violence of the possibility of recovery . . .
this morning, just before Group, looking sour
       Jack weaving from the elevator.

Group

A FEELING Jon is far more anxious for her
sobriety than he says, and more resents
her menace ('If you make me angry, I'll
drink') than he smiles & says.

A feeling they are both resigned to all
that's ill between them & has been & will
for sorry years to come, a 'happy' pair.
'Where's the Serenity Prayer?'

Where sober as you sit here, intimate
in one supreme refraining, full even of love
your privates twitch with theirs under ordeal:
ah Wednesday night is hell.

Each hopeless fear slowly around the circle
gnaws into view, or blurts. Each long-dry throat
still, still with horror & passion runs
immortal alcohols.

Dry Eleven Months

O YES. I've had to give up somewhat here,
illusion on illusion, big books long laboured, a power
of working wellness to some, of securing this house,
the cocktail hour,—
but I am not without a companion: there's left Fear.

I've tried my self, found guilty on each charge
my self diseased. That jury poll was easy;
so was the recommendation, on solid showing
the assassin had been crazy.
But so too were judge & jurors. Now I see sitting large

and sane and near an altogether new
& well advised tribunal. When my ticker stops,
as thrice this fitful year it has done, & re-starts—
each while poor spirit drops
a notch—well, when it quits   for good, I'm afraid of you.

16 December 1971

I DIDN'T. And I didn't. Sharp the Spanish blade
to gash my throat after I'd climbed across
the high railing of the bridge
to tilt out, with the knife in my right hand
to slash me knocked or fainting till I'd fall
unable to keep my skull down but fearless

unless my wife wouldn't let me out of the house,
unless the cops noticed me crossing the campus
up to the bridge
& clappt me in for observation, costing my job—
I'd be now in a cell, costing my job—
well, I missed that;

but here's the terror of tomorrow's lectures
bad in themselves, the students dropping the course,
the Administration hearing
& offering me either a medical leave of absence
or resignation—Kitticat, they can't fire me—

5 Jan 72

Phase Four

I WILL begin by mentioning the word
'Surrender'—that's the 4th & final phase.
The word. What is the thing, well, must be known
in Heaven. 'Acceptance' is the phase before;

if after finite struggle, infinite aid,
ever you come there, friend,
remember backward me lost in defiance,
as I remember those admitting & complying.

We cannot tell the truth, it's not in us.
That truth comes hard. O I am fighting it,
my Weapon One: I know I cannot win,
and half the war is lost, that's to say won.

The rest is for the blessed. The rest is bells
at sundown off across a dozen lawns,
a lake, two strands of laurel, where they come
out of phase three mild toward the sacristy.